Hanukkah at Valley Forge

STEPHEN KRENSKY ✦ illustrated by GREG HARLIN

DUTTON CHILDREN'S BOOKS

◦ DUTTON CHILDREN'S BOOKS ◦
A division of Penguin Young Readers Group

Published by the Penguin Group
Penguin Group (USA) Inc., 375 Hudson Street, New York, New York 10014, U.S.A. • Penguin Group (Canada), 90 Eglinton Avenue East, Suite 700, Toronto, Ontario, Canada M4P 2Y3 (a division of Pearson Penguin Canada Inc.) • Penguin Books Ltd, 80 Strand, London WC2R oRL, England • Penguin Ireland, 25 St Stephen's Green, Dublin 2, Ireland (a division of Penguin Books Ltd) • Penguin Group (Australia), 250 Camberwell Road, Camberwell, Victoria 3124, Australia (a division of Pearson Australia Group Pty Ltd) • Penguin Books India Pvt Ltd, 11 Community Centre, Panchsheel Park, New Delhi—110 017, India • Penguin Group (NZ), Cnr Airborne and Rosedale Roads, Albany, Auckland 1310, New Zealand (a division of Pearson New Zealand Ltd) • Penguin Books (South Africa) (Pty) Ltd, 24 Sturdee Avenue, Rosebank, Johannesburg 2196, South Africa • Penguin Books Ltd, Registered Offices: 80 Strand, London WC2R oRL, England

CIP Data is available.

Published in the United States by Dutton Children's Books,
a division of Penguin Young Readers Group
345 Hudson Street, New York, New York 10014
www.penguin.com/youngreaders

Designed by Jason Henry
Manufactured in China • First Edition
ISBN: 0-525-47738-1

3 5 7 9 10 8 6 4

For Tamar Mays and Steve Meltzer
—SK

To my daughter, Hannah, and to all
future caretakers of history
—GH

EDITOR'S NOTE: Special thanks to Dr. Lee Levine, professor
of Jewish History and Archaeology at the Hebrew University
in Israel, and Rabbi Scott Weiner of The Hebrew Tabernacle
Synagogue in New York, for their invaluable help in recreating
the ancient temple.

The general stood tall on the stony ridge at Valley Forge, surveying his troops below. The December night was clear, but the wind cut cruelly through his heavy coat. The general shook his head, shrugging the cold aside. It was his men he was worried about.

For more than two years his army had been at war. The general had not expected the fighting to be easy. War was never easy. But some of his soldiers lacked weapons to defend themselves. Others were without coats or shoes. And nobody had enough to eat.

"An army of skeletons," one witness had called them.

The snow crunched drily under the general's boots as he walked through the camp. In one crude hut a young soldier was sitting at a small table.

The general watched from the doorway in silence. The soldier was lighting a candle. The flame flickered for a moment and then grew steady. All the while, the soldier was speaking softly, too softly for the general to catch his words.

The general cleared his throat, and the startled soldier jumped up.

"General Washington!" he cried.

His commander in chief nodded. "A cold night, is it not?" he said.

The soldier swallowed nervously. "Truly it is, but no colder than my home back in Poland." He paused. "And there not only is the weather cold, the laws are cold as well. If my family were to light a candle tonight, they would have to do it in secret. But that will not stop them, for this is the first night of Hanukkah."

"Hanukkah?" the general repeated. The word was unfamiliar to him.

"The name for a celebration. I was just finishing a prayer in Hebrew, sir, in honor of what once happened."

"Ah, then you are of the children of Abraham." The general's gaze was intent. "Tell me more of Hanukkah."

The soldier stared at the candle for a moment and then he began to speak.

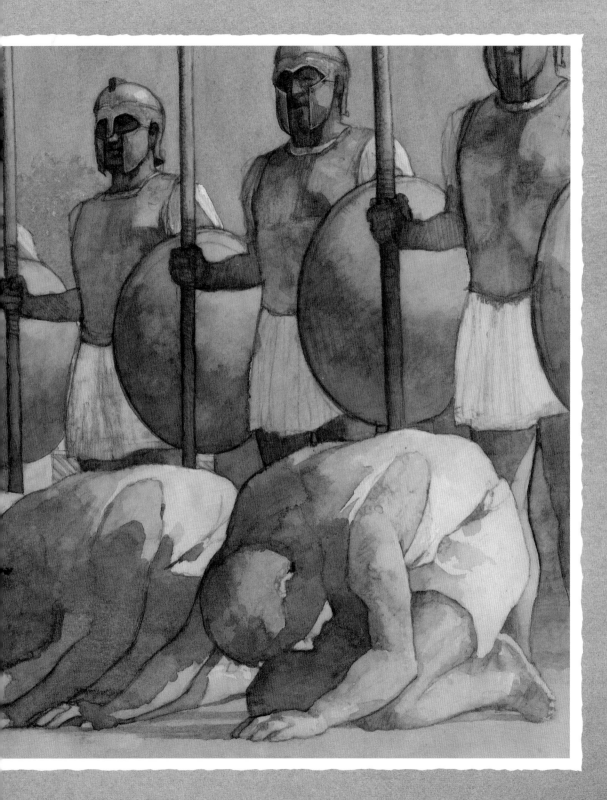

"Over two thousand years ago," said the soldier, "my people, the people of Israel, were ruled by Antiochus, a Greek king from far away. He did not permit them to pray to their god and follow their customs. He wanted them to worship his gods, the Greek gods."

General Washington nodded. "The fight for liberty is an ancient one. And no one likes squirming under the thumb of a distant king."

The soldier looked at his candles. "In my homeland, I could not follow my beliefs either. That is why I came to America."

"But the people of Israel were not so fortunate. In a village near Jerusalem, the soldiers ordered them to bow to the Greek idols and eat from a slaughtered pig. Both of these things were forbidden. In protest, Mattathias, the High Priest, refused to obey. When the ceremony continued without him, he angrily drew his sword. In the fight that followed, lives were lost, though Mattathias escaped.

"He and his five sons, the Maccabees, became the leaders of a rebellion. Some said they were foolish, risking their lives in a doomed cause. But the Maccabees fought on. Their force was small, but they did not give up."

The general sighed. He too was mired in an uphill fight. Independence from England had been declared eighteen months earlier, in July 1776. But declaring it had not ended the war. True, his forces had won some battles, but the British still controlled the major cities and much of the countryside.

"I understand," he said. "We too have a cruel enemy who leaves us only with the choice of brave resistance or abject submission."

"There was one battle," the soldier went on, "where the army of the Maccabees was greatly outnumbered.

"But Mattathias' son Judah rallied their troops. He reminded them that battles are not won or lost solely on strength in the field. 'Our enemies are not invincible,' Judah told them, 'for they trust in arms and acts of daring. But we trust in the Almighty God.'

"Judah and his army won that fight, but many more followed. After three years, though, the Maccabees finally drove their enemies away."

"The Israelites rejoiced in their new freedom and set about cleaning their temple. They were eager to worship again in the ways of their forefathers.

"But when it came time to light the temple menorah, they could find only enough oil to last for one day. That was troubling. Once lit, the menorah was never supposed to go out. Still, they did not want to wait any longer. So they lighted the menorah, trusting that God would help them find more oil as quickly as possible."

"The search for oil was not easy. One day passed quickly, and none was found. Yet the menorah remained lit. Another day went by. Still there was no oil, but the flames remained strong. Three days, four days, the hunt continued. But all the fighting and destruction made finding things very difficult. In all, eight days passed before any new oil arrived.

"And in all that time, the lights of the menorah never went out."

The soldier blew on his hands to warm them. "Truly a miracle happened there. So every year we remember this festival of lights. Tonight is the first night of Hanukkah, and therefore I lit only the first candle of the Hanukkah menorah, the *Hanukkiah*. I will use this special candle, the *Shamash*, to light one candle each night until there are eight. Eight candles to honor the eight days the oil lasted."

The general made ready to leave. "Your tale is a brave one. And your candles have brightened my evening. Perhaps we are not as lost as our enemies would have us believe. I rejoice in the Maccabees' success, though it is long past." He smiled grimly. "And it pleases me to think that miracles may still be possible."

The soldier nodded. "The world would be a poor place without them."

"So it would," said General Washington, with a lighter mood than he had felt in many a day. As he continued on his rounds, the wind quieted, and the Hanukkah candles burned long into the night. ∼

AUTHOR'S NOTE

~

This story of George Washington and Hanukkah is based on facts, but the tale itself must be taken on faith. It is known that in December 1778, Washington had lunch at the home of Michael Hart, a Jewish merchant in Easton, Pennsylvania (cited in Jacob Rader Marcus's *United States Jewry 1776–1985*). It was the middle of Hanukkah, and when Hart began to explain the holiday to the general, Washington replied that he knew it already. He then told the merchant and his family of meeting the Polish soldier at Valley Forge the year before. It was Hart's stepdaughter Louisa who reportedly committed the story to her diary (which was later recounted in Rabbi I. Harold Sharfman's book *Jews on the Frontier*).

Since Washington himself kept no diary during the war years, he left no personal record of the event. Certainly, though, the story fits in with the curiosity and reactions Washington displayed on later occasions. In that spirit, some of Washington's dialogue here has been borrowed from his own writings in the hope of echoing his real voice.